THE OTHER DOOR

POEMS & GLIMPSES

MARY LOU MCAULEY

THE OTHER DOOR PRESS

Copyright © 2015 by Mary Lou McAuley
All rights reserved

The Other Door Press
955 Clatsop Avenue
Astoria, OR 97103

Grateful acknowledgement is made to *North Coast Squid*, 2015 No. 4, for publication of "River Paths" and "Night Spell."

Cover image: "Escape," oil on panel, plein air by Robert Paulmenn

ISBN: 978-0-692-36616-5

For Robert

CONTENTS

PART I

The Other Door	1
River Time – View from the Crest Motel	2
The Shell	3
Dressed to Go Out	4
Starlight	5
Self Portrait	6
Geode	7
No McDonald's Corporate Farm	8
Dusk	9
Summer Wasps	10
Obedience	11
Go	12
Taking	13
Origin Myth	14
Home Movies	15
Night Swimmer	16
Cougar Waltz	17
The Lie Dreaming You	18
The Orchard Ghost	19
The Tailor	20
The Orange Coat	21
Racing with a Storm	22
I Can't	23
Before	24
Definition	25
Demon Racing	26
Night Spell	27
Button Moon	30
God Is Blowing Bubbles	31
The Sun's Hand	32
Out of the Cradle	33
An Introduction	34

Flying Lesson	35
When Leaves Can Play	36
Wild Trilliums	37
Another Poet Said	38
Passing By	39
Wish	40
Web Mending	41
Recital	42
Steptoe Butte	43
Call and Response	44
Who Took That Picture	45
Spring Walk	46
Just Let It Go: A Mini Memoir in Third Person Singular	47
Thinking of War	49
Corpse Shadow: Hiroshima	50
The Knife Maker	51
Lullaby Moon	52

PART II

The Real Gate	55
Thirteen	56
"Over"	60
Open the Door of Your Longing	61
First Sight	62
Jazz Club	63
Camptown Races	64
Thaw	65
Coveting	66
I Would Know You Better	68
A Cradle Song	69
Age's Dream	70
Fractions	71
Pick Me	72
Inkwell of Light	73

The Road Home	74
Weather Change	75
Shipyard Lunch	76
Detour	77
River Walker	78
Get Out of My Way	79
Asylum	80
Glimpses	81
Following	82
Chrysalis	83
Lost & Found	84
Sunday's Best	85
The Library Steps	86
Workshop	87
Yoo-Hoo!	88
The Snyders' Goat	89
Running with Robert	90
I Brought Back Sounds	91
Tsunami	92
Marilyn	93
River Paths	94
Declarations	95
River of Permission	96
Acknowledgements	99

Memory believes before knowing remembers.
–William Faulkner
Light in August

PART I

THE OTHER DOOR

When you wrote that
I felt, of course, that you wrote that
just for me.
I thought, Oh good,
I thought you were helping me,
explaining something,
easing my timidity.
In a dark room, perhaps another's light
can show the way out.
But light borrowed from another
leaves with them.
Now I know, you really were speaking to me
and what you were trying to tell me:
I am the other door.

River Time – View from the Crest Motel

What would it be like to live down there?
October with an early leaf fire smoldering,
the season's first pale smoke.
Pumpkins set in a row, awaiting the knife.
A sighing, sagging fence,
is pulled down lower by dead grasses, damp and heavy.
Distant sun and darts of shadow
stitch the sloping back yard seam
toward the river.
But the river knows what it is like to live down there.
Aware of railroad ties and sharp gravel,
painted rusty pores, the river ships,
keenly hearing the seal barks,
and gulls, and even the slow motion tread of that heron.
Seeing out of the corner of its millions of eyes, a dragonfly
cutting mysterious corners, knows the algae in that marsh
shallow has added another square foot.
My molecules might register as a particle or a wave,
or the way a breeze shimmies the surface, but no more than that.
I am too porous to rest in this river.
I would slip through her fingers
the way the afternoon shadow slips through my arm
and finds itself on the other side of the table and
without clinging,
slips off, down the bank, and into the water where
it is known as time.

THE SHELL

The fragment of a shattered snail shell
was right where I was about to put my hand
on the warm stone bench.
So fragile, the small piece,
inner ribs still pearly with pale hints of the columns
holding the ancient memory of form.
And there, right on top of the curve
had walked an ant
and that ant by some seeping glue
stands where it stuck and died,
on the edge of a winding gold shell
like a victor astride a bronze horse.

Dressed to Go Out

A string of pearls
a black silk dress with a shimmering wrap
that is the attire of the storm moving toward us.
With snow geese circling the pale neck of sky,
black silk clouds burdened by the mountain's generosity
push the silver wrap
away
and it waves back as lightning.
The strand of pearls breaks apart
and pearly geese disappear under the furniture of trees
while the black dress is shed
for a clean blue one.

STARLIGHT

In the night of this
strange place
my senses seek a familiar view
but it is the starlight
through the dark darkness that guides me.
Moths navigate by starlight
in the darkness they seek their way
but fingers of light beckon them
earthward
waiting to steal their wings.

SELF PORTRAIT

How unlikely
the magician showing the trick
as he bends the light
away from the mirror
toward himself
and away again
as paint

Geode

Geode
ancient, formed perfect
crusted by earth's extraordinary, porous skin
creating lights in beauty's darkness
with no yearning to be set free
but time in this world keeps track
of seasons
until frost's great cracking release
pushes one globe
that falls to shattering below
and everything bows at the breaking
high stars swell in the
crystal reflection
and the sun
when she wakes
finds her table littered
with jewels

No McDonald's Corporate Farm

Antoine de Saint-Exupery
wrote of what would happen
to penned ducks or chickens
when the seasonal wild migrations began.
They would leap about
magnetically drawn to the great
tug of instinct and memory.
Do they still?
I doubt it,
because
now they are packed tight
in small cages
no leaping room at all.
In constantly lighted rooms
their eyes may as well be stitched shut.
For them there is no sunlight, no starlight.
They drink through lopsided beaks
but only measured food
designed to speed
their destined cycle.
Whoever thought we could desire
to feed ourselves on such misery
and have health?
Find a real farm,
when wild migrations are above you,
where a hen at least has a chance to leap,
invite yourself to dinner,
you may taste starlight.

Dusk

Sometimes a sip of wine
at dusk
will bring the shadows of words I have reached for all day.
I know then I have given up too easily.
Those syllables, curves and dots have been waiting for me
to let them suck the ink from my pen.
So, sometimes a sip of wine
at dusk,
between the inhale and exhale
between the constant chatter of familiar words,
I glimpse the texture and color,
the fold or the scale,
and I hurry to offer those shadows
my pen.

Summer Wasps

The dripping leaves
release the summer shower
tracing the strong leaf vein
gathering to a starred orb at the tip
that drops,
and the elegant mud-daubing wasps
singly come
hovering at the slowly receding edges of the dark
newborn puddle.
Like expert waiters
they reach carefully and quickly
bending to the water
lifting each drop back into the sky.

OBEDIENCE

Two dogs were playing next door
bumping, tumbling, hind leg chewing
then the big one started a loud laugh
the way dogs do
and he was immediately sent
to his high fenced back yard room.
Expressions of joy are lost
in the fenced rooms of obedience.

Go

The wind leaned into me the night I decided to leave.
My cells seemed to realign themselves,
letting the fingers of wind pass through me,
like I was just a feather on the wing of a bird.
So I turned toward my ocean room.
The seven miles of sand I had paced
the way some pace a carpeted, familiar room.
There were times in that pacing
when I would enter pockets of great sorrow
and sometimes gladness,
and I knew I walked along an altar of sand.
It was a day of funhouse mirrors,
the day I decided to leave,
so I turned to my old friend the sea
I stepped to the altar
and the wind pressed into me and said
"Now."

Taking

The bright muscular arm of the Columbia River stunned my sight by its breadth. Whirlpools looking the size of saucers in reality could spin and drown a boat. The Celilo fishing platforms were there and then no more. Sunday drives would take us to Horsethief Lake where we could pick up pails full of arrowheads. When my grandmother's room was finally accessible after her death, we found rows of cotton lined boxes holding the agate shapes of tiny spears. I took one out and thumbed its fluted ridges and thought of the delicacy and intent of its shape. Was this one for a bird? A fish? I knew so little of the treasure I had looted from the timeline I had interrupted. Sometimes we would stop at the Maryhill Museum. The large downstairs chambers once housed the stable and many fine horses. Their bays now used for glass cases of woven baskets, dolls, fragments of attire and shoes. Still. Stopped in time, designed to be part of a seasonal cycle, they no longer knew their way. I felt sad looking at the facsimiles of villages or habits, and now I know why. Like taxidermy they were the hollow vessel without the being, time interrupted by what is missing, not lost, but taken out. Arrowheads, fishing platforms, watering holes. There came a time when a chain link fence was put around our arrowhead hunting ground and we grumbled at being prevented from taking buckets full of what was really not ever ours to touch.

Origin Myth

Deeply laid in memory and the veiling of innocent hope
are the stories of our origin.
The memories are fed by how we imagine
anything and everything
could have happened just as it did.
The acts of others, though, are never experienced fully by us,
but our own experiences of having and losing,
succeeding and failing
or breaking inside,
all shade with forgiveness the stories we have come to believe.

Home Movies

Hoisting up the large, white, bumpy screen, my grandfather locked it in place and started threading the film through the projector. In my memory we were always sitting on the large couch, leaning forward, eager. Movie night was a special event.

My grandmother is shoveling snow in the jerky rapid movements of 8mm black-and-white film. My mother's hand holds a paper in front of the camera that reads "1949." Then bundled to my chin, arms sticking straight out from my sides in a tightly packed snow suit, I am carried out to the snow on the front yard. My sister and I stand together, gleeful confusion registers on what can be seen of our squeezed faces.

Adult hands and arms reach into the frame, my sister looks up and in a brief ruffle of light showing through film sprockets we're together again running and jumping through the sprinkler in white July sun. Then our dog, then a flower, then our car, then me. The last frame is no longer black and white and I am no longer two. And that was the end of my home movie career.

Night Swimmer

I am a night swimmer
drawn to dark water
to glide through the frail
lace of moonlight.
No sunlight splashes
disturb the surface
above is the same as below.
My arms look less human
my hair a water weed,
there is no distance to shore
for all is water
reflection or reality
they are the same
and each stroke brings
me no nearer to one or the other.

Cougar Waltz

In my dream I found myself rearing up and embracing a large cougar-like cat, in a step-to-step parody of someone trying to disarm a knife wielding intruder: back step back, side step side, slide, slide, slide.

When I was a child I was told the story of a young girl being dragged from her front porch by a cougar, (mainly to make me come in after dark), but I refused to believe she had died. So I had adopted a cougar as my invisible companion, protector and knew she would walk with me when I went into the dark woods. Huge paws that slightly flipped with each step, I could almost feel her warm side up against me. But as often happens, her companionship faded long ago. So when I thought about my dream today, I wondered: had she come back to kill me or to ask me to dance?

The Lie Dreaming You

Life falls short sometimes
short of dreams or
prospects or promises.
Places you move to lie
about themselves.
And you wake up one day
and the first person you meet
says just some small thing
and you know.
You haven't awakened at all.
You are still asleep
and the lie
is dreaming you.

THE ORCHARD GHOST

My sleepy moving shadow lingers
until sounds rally my drifting focus.
A wind chime, bruising gentle air to sing,
a young crow, helpless and insistent.
There is a memory of where I am,
where I have been,
what I carried.
Other dreams have remembered a different place,
a road now where once a river was,
a tooth of chimney where once an orchard
exhaled perfume and rot and bees.
There is something I intended to do here,
perhaps I buried what I carried.
And with that thought, the orchard ghost says,
as the wind chime shatters and the crow calls my name,
the orchard ghost says,
witch it up.
Witch it up with your bones.

THE TAILOR

High on the bluff
shadowed animal tracks in the snow draw my eye.
Precise perforations mark
the landscape's shoulder,
small stitches nick the padded folds of snow.
With ease this tailor shows how the fabric is cut
and skillfully hides the seam between the rocks.

The Orange Coat

Wearing an orange coat
with her dancer's stride
she blows down the sidewalk
like every young wind
red hair sparking the
candle of her slim body.
Forty years ahead
she waits,
stands,
in a pale down jacket,
knit hat pulled low, brown slacks
high at the ankle.
Two loaded plastic sacks
bear down on curved fingers
but pinch no ring.
She waits with her burden
for the light to change
orange to white
she crosses.

Racing with a Storm

When the rain began it started as fat drops, clear liquid marbles cratering the red dust on the hood of the car. Dark low clouds added volume to the flow until the wipers' struggle to slosh the water off the windshield threatened to pull them from their housing. To my right, slicing beneath the iron filings of ragged cloud, a skein of geese flew, flung like spray from a midnight fountain. I felt I could be with them, flying, suspended in the wingbeat of the storm, the roar of the wet tires like a new kind of wind. The hood of the car was glistening, the trunk dry. The geese pulled up and banked away from my sight and then the rain hit the trunk. Just for a moment I straddled what the geese divided. Storm clouds, wind, rain, wings.

I Can't

Failure to begin
already believing it is too late to try,
pocket-patting the emotional suit, you say,
Oh, yes, too late, I can't.
So now it is true
and walking to the other side of the room
alone in a chair
you sit
as others file in to share with you
their reasons
all the ways they are soothed by the word:
unable.

BEFORE

To move into new skin
the old must be shed
the pulling off
so necessary
so risky
and the eyes watch
and the mouth says
not yet
and the mind has fled in panic.
But the eyes that know no mirror
see what has always been there.
Beneath the skin,
is the before the skin.
Change is nothing at all.

DEFINITION

What the hell is a 'subverted sonnet'?
I am in the wrong place.
"Refer to Glossary"
"A poem whose form is determined by the numbers
of syllables in the lines. Syllables are read with sense stress
rather than metric stress, and there is no necessary pattern
of stresses."
I take it back. I'm free.

Demon Racing

The shadow of the car, rounded like the shape of a crouched animal raced me from the ditch, wavering, leaping forward, falling down, full again with a snout, then with ears, then just a blurring at a curve; a demon animal, racing me. I couldn't resist a sideways glance. Don't look at it! I lightly tapped the brakes, thinking to stop, to test the fear and the thrill at the same time. Dark miles in either direction yet something deep in my imagination was believing I was being tracked by a wild shadow. Reckless in a boldness I wasn't completely in agreement with, I pulled the car to the side of the road, left the car running and the door open and stepped to the ditch. Okay, I will look at you! I will see you! I really need this magic!

Just a ditch, murky with puddles backed up behind slimed weeds and old cans shining, this was not a stream that would ever truly flow. Its nature was to slowly seep through the pores of the ground to become the dark perfumed atmosphere of moles and sightless damp.

Backing away I returned to the car. Of course the crouching shadow sprang forward as I steered the car back toward town. I lost it there. But that didn't matter: It knew I saw it.

NIGHT SPELL

On an August night in 1992, I returned to a high plateau above the Columbia River. Crossing a cattle guard I pulled my car just into the fence line and got out. Placing the toe tip of my boot on the bottom strand of wire, I bent low, rolled past the sharp barbs of tight wire and walked until I could no longer see any lights across the river.

The field where I walked was once well known to me. Some miles away, a ranch house nestled in a grove of shading trees, surrounded by the ten thousand acre ranch that belonged to the family of my best friend. It was impossible for me, a kid who measured distance by the block, to grasp the vast holding of what really appeared to be only horizon. But it was that very horizon and a moment one summer night over thirty years before that I had come to reclaim.

A well-worn path was easy to see; cattle had followed each other from the rickety pens at the road, in single file, to the open pasture above. Soon, the one path became many and cresting a small rise, I entered the open night. A whispering wind combed the dry grasses and sage coaxing the kind of conversation from the ground that can twirl a body in circles, head swiveling, looking for the speakers. Savoring the jitters, I was watchful and alert. As I stood that night to call down the stars and invoke my own spell of memory, I realized how this landscape had shaded my heart. Like an orphan duckling following high barnyard boots, when I left this place it followed me. Its curves and contours and the bright muscle of the Columbia below had never left me.

My friend and I had been out riding and the afternoon was already giving the long warning shadows of dusk and dark. When we got to the flat top of the last hill before the descent to the ranch, Melissa flicked her heels in the stirrups and called back over her shoulder "Race ya!"

Star, the sweet tempered mare that carried me, played along for a while but her gallop soon turned into a lope that could have been a rocking chair or a speed-steadied train. Rhythm, the percussion of her hooves was the cadence of our breath. Hoofbeats, leather creaking, a sting of mane on my cheek, closer, closer to her neck I bent down, closer my left hand on her neck, closer, her deep summer horse smell, closer her breath not beneath me but my own. Stretched out we ran in place, the earth, the rough sage and dark ground barely touched by her feet. Ahead of us straight horizon, pinned by bright winking stars. I can clearly see the leather shine of the bridle across her starred forehead, its straps soft along her cheeks and jaw to the bit and the reins, reins held loosely in my hand, unneeded for guidance. We are in a fume of the smell of sage and dust and rocks that crack beneath each metal shoe. Her lope creates the concussion of each hoof to the leg, to the shoulder, to my center that is spread across her back in a leather seat that is worn and soft, a conduit to a human soul. From Star's spine sparks must surely have been shooting up into me, threads of the invisible that write and rewrite this moment again and again. Those sparks settled in my spine and so too the starlight, the bruised sage. Flying, together we are wild.

Then a yellow glow lighted Star's ears and the back of my hands. Fast rising, full and laughing, the moon rose on my left, straight up over the rim of the plateau, close to the ground and bullying by its size. That immense August moon seemed so big and round and close and flat that I could have fisted its rims and pulled it down to my head like a hat. That was the night I came here to remember and renew, somehow to always feel that wild gallop.

The moon at last was coming up, and I began to breathe in the night. Out, beyond me, in the pale light, I knew I saw a horse in mid-stride, a girl stretched forward, and then they faded as the light grew, and I was again alone beneath the stars.

Whispering shadows followed me back to the car and I felt even edgier, like I had disturbed something powerful with my wishful prayer. I smelled sage as my boots once again stepped on the path. Getting back to my car, I stood a moment and looking down at the river. I smiled. I had done what I wanted; I had looked for something older that held the magic of shape and power and memory. I had invited it to somehow stay with me and let that young girl and horse keep traveling the plateau.

A small pebble, lodged in the heel of my boot scratched the hallway tile when I walked into the house. It fell as I raised my foot. Picking it up, rolling it and tossing it in my palm, just before I slipped it into my pocket, I pictured where I had been standing hours before when I saw myself galloping by. And there it was, clear as a bell. Some magic had come home with me after all.

Button Moon

Tonight the full moon rose up through
the clouds
like a button fastening a sleeve.
Such a lovely hint.
There will be snow in the morning.

God Is Blowing Bubbles

So look at it this way:
God is blowing bubbles.
You are just the sheen on the bubble before it bursts.
Not even the whole bubble.
Not even the drops that fall.
Just a quick iridescent sheen.
Only designed to go so far, so high.
Designed to burst.

The Sun's Hand

I longed to see the sun
and it came
in its own time.
Not as a dazzle in a wide open blue
but as a fist of light
slamming the trees against a gunmetal sky,
opening itself to reflective ripples
its palm shining in water
at my feet.

Out of the Cradle

I thanked Walt for whispering
". . . endlessly rocking."
I needed to hear that
to be deaf to the shouting of this world.
A thousand pelicans? Six hundred gulls?
Infinite, uncountable grains of sand.
To spend a day not counting,
not naming,
just letting Walt whisper:
"out of the cradle endlessly rocking."

An Introduction

I am soft
no angles to bump into.
I am transparent but tending
to gray and brown.
I am one dimensional, flat
not even able to curl or ripple,
I am strong, spread wide,
I adhere.
I am regret.

FLYING LESSON

Geese flying low
no formation
all battling a strong, high wind I do not yet feel
they seem tossed, unruly and then I notice
one is larger
sharing its knowledge in strong flight and voice
"we try" the others call back
but one, far below them
looks up, twists in its turn
and finds the lesson.

When Leaves Can Play

The leaves
no longer the green webbed palms of summer
shake loose and tumble against the thick brown ankles of trees.
Then pry free to run across their parents roots
and pad noisily down the dark October road
to chase a jumpy walker.
They grin as they whirl way up over the meadow
where they too have desired the kiss
of flower flirting butterflies.
When the wind begins to see their cracks and veins
it carries them back to where they started
lays them down
and whispers: "Next Year?"

Wild Trilliums

I had been in the deep cedar woods,
found them where faint sunlight warmed,
gathered them all as a present.
Mother's hand quickly covered her mouth
her eyes squinted as though she smelled vinegar.
You see, I had picked every flower
in the deep cedar woods.
"Seven years," my grandmother whimpered, head down
the whup-whup of the screen door closing
didn't cover my mother's gasp,
"If ever."

Another Poet Said

He must have believed
that part where he talks about
eternity running wild in the streets.
I read the poem many times
a challenge
looking for falseness, a lie.
And, at last I found it,
the lie.
It was the one I'd been telling myself.

Passing By

On the way to BiMart I often drove out of my way on the curving road that took me past the horses. Four, sometimes five horses grazed across the sloping meadow and were usually, by their timing of the day, near the fence that paralleled the road when I drove by.

Early fall at times can look like early spring; bristles of tall grasses or weeds can look either like winter is coming or winter is going, the shade of green in the grass, too could belong to any season. So in the late October afternoon sunlight I was thinking of spring and seeing the horses. A paint, a bay, a buckskin. Then in a slow motion movement as I turned my head, the tall bay took a step and I was looking at his sun-starred muscular shoulder. Each muscle was defined in the extension of his step, each muscle opened and closed and pulled and let go. He bent his neck to graze. I followed a curve, and that was all.

Wish

A wish came to me
from another world,
a world where I had walked upon
its back and leaned upon
dark ribs.
But I could not recognize it
although it was a clear, almost visible thing.
And a time came when, once in a canyon,
I almost glimpsed its garments,
but that was only a trick of light.
When in my sleep I heard it whisper,
I turned over and sighed,
that is just the wind.
So the wish keeps vigil,
an extra hour chimed on the
striking clock,
a piece of verse fluttering out
of a dusty book.
Hoping I'll notice
in spite of distractions.
Waiting to hear me say
I remember you.

Web Mending

This morning I watched a spider
move briskly
with one or two jerky stops
across the siding
and then just as quickly
without stopping
vanish again into a crack.
A spider looks only for gaps in its web
like the Grand Idea
its existence depends on its prepared concealment,
its discovery usually fatal.

Recital

The curtains open and I walk out.
Through bright blindness I see
dust motes swirl in the stage lights.
There is an odor of fabric
and dust and polish.
In a dizzying moment, my brain erases
but somehow
a melody becomes familiar.
The conductor points to me
and between the notes
just before I begin
to let me know she is there
I hear my mother cough.

Steptoe Butte

Just off the highway I found the overgrown entrance to the campground. Steptoe Butte. Closed. The picnic table was on its side, the chained garbage cans upside down and lidless, a toilet building with a scarred and faded door, made secure in all the disarray by a bolted square of bright metal. My dog Banjo and I stepped over a broken sign and looked into the deep fir shade and turned back to the idling truck. I would have liked to eat there but there was no welcome in that place, and the bordering forest skirt looked so dark and tattered it seemed to be haunted. So I decided to drive up to the top of the Butte. Up, up and around and up again, I followed the narrow spiral of pavement but could not see the road past the hood of the Chevy. My hands tightened on the wheel at each curve and my foot took on a quaking pulse as I trusted the low gear to take us forward and still up. And then, we were at the top. Far below I could see cattle and fields fading in the draping dusk, tiny bales of hay throwing house-size shadows. And with a heart leap, I realized we were not alone at the top of Steptoe Butte. The guard rail post directly to my left suddenly split apart and its top opened to a wing spread of copper and speckle. The hawk toe-pushed off the rail and without any wing movement, drifted past our astonished gazes, broke into open air and showed us her fine back and red tail.

CALL AND RESPONSE

Rumi's words
softly lift the hair
from the bell of my ears,
and my own bell answers,
calling myself to worship
not correctly
but often.

Who Took That Picture

There she sits. Such a great picture. Slim, thoughtful, she gives the camera her left profile, her right hand supporting her chin. The photograph appears to have been taken through an open classroom door. Weighing down the right margin is the edge of a black board. Tight in, with a magnifying glass, I have decided the writing there to be in her distinguished hand. The month and the year, and a partial sentence that could be a reading assignment.

There must be windows across from where she sits because her blouse is blurred from the glare of light on the film, exaggerated by the boundaries of the door frame and her dark suit jacket. So, glowing and silent she waits there for my curiosity.

My mother's first teaching assignment was at the Nez Perce Reservation in Ione, Washington. It would be many, many years before she met my father. But this picture feels intimate, loving. I wonder of course about her life then, her days and friends. But, mostly, I wonder: Who took that picture?

Spring Walk

All should walk with an old slow dog in late spring.
Turning the familiar corner
see where lilacs lean over the gray wood fence
and there your companion will pause
and you can inhale the fragrance
the collection of each pale flower
and see it exhale bees from its heavy tall blossoms.
It is one long drink of perfume.
Farther along there are big-headed tulips
with glossy bright petals shaped like shoe horns.
Heading home it seems the hum of the bees
grows louder and you remember:
lawns, hoses, daisies, laughter, the slap
of slamming screen doors,
and the sun-burned boys of summer
growing their new round muscles
by embracing bales of hay.

Just Let It Go: A Mini Memoir in Third Person Singular

The ache keeps her faithful. It has to be worth it because it is all she has lived for. The ache gives her purpose to come and wait for more words.

Returning to the library she becomes more aware of the pressure in her chest. She knows it is full of words but she is belligerent about the naming, concentrating instead on the shift and shape of the feeling. It could be organic, a personal system failure, but she believes it is the weight of the space taken up by words. Thousands of them.

The library's hushed atmosphere helps her concentrate, listening with fetal ear buds, no one can see that she is trying to hear a feeling. The room is bright with florescent lights. Other's eyes and hands are busy in exchanging symbols for meaning. Letters and dots for ideas and vision. She imagines the noise possible if she opened an atlas. With one more scan of the room, she takes a moment to look at the giant chessboard with its medieval pieces shaped like castles, knights, queens and kings, all molded in black and white plastic. There is a white piece invading the black line and a black piece avenging on the white side. That war appears to have been abandoned. How long before another attack begins?

The sensation in her chest is moving again, lifting upward. She pictures coils and knots of words pulsing, flowing. In her waiting has the vacancy caused a suction to pull what she is waiting for up and out? She hopes she will not scream whenever it exits. She almost expects pain. Maybe this is what birth is and death. We own neither, they come to us and we fill up the spaces in between. Fill them quickly without waiting for the rest. The confusion of all our different schooling kicks in and we see possibilities as facts. But we never were taught to wait for the rest. Thinking clouds the sky of our life. Thoughts rushing across the days like things blown. Of course, we don't see the wind and so concentrate on the clouds alone. Their height, direction, color, beauty, threat. Mere drops of moisture that evaporate and shift and disappear make up most of our thoughts. So the sensation she is waiting to deliver ties in somehow. The emptying of the clouds of thoughts, feels like the end of a certain kind of gravity. An untethered sensation she does not like but cannot summon anything else to hold on to, only a sudden onset of weary fatigue.

The library has a courtyard and she rests her head on folded arms. She sees all this afternoon's waiting and listening take the form of a boat, its shape familiar. It is holding her life and memories and longing and dread. It has felt leaky for a long time and trying to keep it afloat she just piled more into it. In the sunny drowse, a confidence whispers to her: "Just let it go. Let it wallow and slip away." Faint and quiet it is her own voice coming from the knot in her chest. So she lets the boat slip away, lay over on its side, drift in slow motion down, to rest and rock on the bottom of the stream. All the cargo, all just tipping out and cartwheeling away. Ink bleeds pale color into the current, water grasses carefully turn aside a page, smiling snapshots give wrinkled grins to the sand and gravel. Look at all she had crammed onto that once small, proud boat. Ghost memories and old songs, shoes that took her feet nowhere, the old tires of promises, blown out and flat. Bags of sand once needed to prevent drift now escape to their own beginnings. Air bubbles here and there, like whispers released from the planks of wood, scoot and wiggle to the surface where they too give up the confinement of spaces that held them. Dreaming she looks on and wonders where the boat went down. Was it there? There? Shouldn't there be a gap in the water to even briefly show its passing? Her craft, forbidden to move by knowledge, expectation its tether. Out of sight and empty it is free. Now it can go anywhere.

The blare of a horn wakes her. Bewildered she gathers her notebooks and walks toward the street. Longing never prepares you for its departure.

Thinking of War

Just over there, shadowed, stained and overgrown
are buildings that continue to haunt me.
I trespass to explore them.
Crunching through wrecked window frames,
around groves of rebar
that look like ferns under a killing spell,
my feet tumble bricks hemmed with their failed mortar
scabbed with white paint, starred at the corners from falling.
In rusted shades they are scattered across the floor
as though they had been hurled
from one side of the building to the other.
Once, grasses had found their way into this inhospitable land,
and in spite of their young green reaching and squeezing
they died standing,
full of seed.

Corpse Shadow: Hiroshima

Stare transfixed
a light so bright
ten thousand suns
creating
ten thousand shades of shadow
as though nicked
from the the stones
shadow prised
from the light
the shape
of someone just going home

The Knife Maker

The knife maker is coming
she is hunting
to find the best use for her blade.
Immune to your insistence
that she should wait
she moves indifferent through your shadow.
She knows your path has been seeded by
lookalikes, with your backward glancing
might have beens.
She knows you still want to sleep.
But the knife maker is coming
and she can't be slowed
her swift advance full of purpose.
Remember, she is the help you called for
and she will visit you and leave you totally alone.
The knife maker is coming, she knows the best use for her blade.
She is harvesting dead memories and cherished regret
and on her belt she carries her harvest.
A regret is the pelt of a trapped memory.
The knife maker is coming.

Lullaby Moon

Pre-dawn the first morning and I stood on the porch of the cabin in unfamiliar darkness, eyes blinking, wide open, light starved. The nearby river spoke in a deep belling language I did not know, a night bird called out just once, and I was aware of how tame I had become. To my right, I sensed, without really seeing, a slightly deeper dent in the darkness. It moved. A smacking sound stirred my straining nerves and I realized it was a bear. A bear eating fallen apples, following its own star-lighted, apple scented familiar path, while I stood breath-holding still.

    The four of us on the retreat knew there was a bear that wandered along the river and near the cabin, and those who rose early kept a loose journal of when we saw her. Each morning, the darkness became less solid for me and each morning I could recognize some constellations, and then, as one cured of an old blindness, I could also see the ridge, the stand of pine trees, the trunks of the apple trees. So much life was moving around me in those dark early mornings, bear size, mouse size, winged. My ears, too, opened and the sound of the river became more defined and I could sense a pulse as earth's heart poured liquid through the canyon vein. Wild turkeys came through and a coyote's voice called, tricking my sense of direction with the breeze.

    To get to the cabin from where we parked our cars we needed to cross a suspension bridge, a span held together by planks and cables and engineering wisdom. Crossing the bouncy, swaying bridge it was easy to feel the suspension of my life, crossing between one life and another. It was not a sharp delineation, but the blurry edges of time spent by clocks, by distance covered by tires, by vigil in front of the blue screen of networks. The household left, the familiar landscape of street lights and sidewalks, not gone or forgotten, just away. Time reformed and put on the garments of light and shadow, the difference of dusk and dawn, the transparent green of late afternoon sun on the tallest trees.

So the days passed from meals to writing to fireside and fragrant smoke, to the slow emptying of the living room, to the one-by-one darkening of the house, to again, a bear coming to eat apples by starlight.

She did not visit us on that last night, while we polished our eyes with moonlight, taking pictures of the full moon as it came over the canyon rim, shadowed by just the fingertips of what would be a late fall storm. Perhaps she smelled the high moisture of coming snow, and full of sweet apples was already thinking of sleep, following the chime of her ancient blood's clock.

We drove away, leaving the canyon our laughter, the smells of our food offerings, our gazes, and the suspension bridge to bounce and sway only by the wind's running feet. But always, now when I look up and see the full moon in late October I think of it as the moon who calls those who must leave back to their own beds, and those who must stay to deep canyon dreams: Always it will be the Lullaby Moon of the Imnaha.

PART II

The Real Gate

I wonder if our own memories are clotted or thinned by the overbearing imaginations of those we knew, the shaping laboratory of family myths, traditions. Those times were lived by those who came before me and stepping into that filament, that web, and without knowing a single thing, I began to store memories of everything. So we must search for our story.

Maybe we go back to our beginnings like a poor wanderer carrying hand-me-down gifts. Holding tight to anonymous bundles of memories that we have been told are our own. But if we agree to take them we might wander past the real gate, mistaking their terrain as our own.

Thirteen

Sometimes the pieces of our lives just seem out of place. Like a cracked and buckled sidewalk, not only do the pieces no longer fit but other organisms have taken up residence between the cracks. We look up at the big, looming tree right next to the heaved cement, we look down to the ground where the root system has bent and shoved its joints to the air and say, well, the tree caused this. As a child I thought a firm stomp on the highest point would just put everything back in its place. The puzzle was something to be fixed, smoothed and restored. I've spent many years stomping on my own puzzles seeking to fix this, smooth that. But unlike jig saw puzzles, life's pattern has no border and all the pieces don't necessarily fit.

Everything in my life that year was only sort of working. Our marriage had ended and my husband and I agreed that I would take the truck and go on a road trip. I had used all the current cliches to justify yet another sad disruption in that good man's life. I wanted to find a place, in fact I was sure I would find a place where I would suddenly fit in, and by that longed-for comfort be suddenly inspired. In an old Chevy pickup with a camper top, my dog Banjo and I headed east. Although I had stalled myself for at least a month, moving through geography seemed to be the only way of honestly saying good bye.

Following mainly secondary roads, I spent most of the days taking the trip in small pieces. Quiet rest stops fed me vistas of movement and the wide open stretches of eastern Washington gave me the lifting sense of possibilities. But on the second day, the counting began. I talked to my dog, played some music and then the counting. One, two, three, four. Over and over the same numbers. I would catch myself, stop myself and say aloud: "What?" What is up with this counting? Nothing came immediately to mind and a few more miles down the road, the counting would start again.

Through Idaho and into Montana the old truck carried us. I got lost a couple of times, but it was easy to back track, to keep going east. One time I pictured my truck as a small game board piece, pushed by an unseen finger along a colored, striped roadway about to be stopped at the next square. I looked at other cars I met, trying to picture their invisible finger friends. And then I was counting again, and, I was adding more numbers. One, two, three, four, five, six, seven, eight. One, two, three. Stop!

The word 'psychosis' entered my mind. I had been under a self-imposed strain. Pulling apart a marriage still too new to see failure from the start. I already knew and hid that ball of knowing like a bruise, until nothing could cover the obvious. I wanted out. And leaving, I did in a truck what my cowardice couldn't voice. One, two, three, four, on up to eight.

I camped by rivers, followed Nez Perce ghosts, fled in advance of a howling storm. With my hands on the wheel I would glance over and meet Banjo's steady gaze. Maybe he was just hoping for another stop, but in the cab of that truck I read his every look as a question. Of the two of us, only he knew that we would be doing this again and again. One, two, three, four, five, six, seven, eight.

When we reached Livingston, I rented a motel room, bought some wine and diner food. And for the next week I laid on the bed watching television. The weather mostly. I was depressed and bored. What, what was I doing? The emptiness and disappointment of my arrival seeped into my heart. I didn't come to Montana, I left Washington. I tried some exploring and shopping, but every day I saw the snow line on the closest mountains drop lower and lower. I guess I really wanted to stay in the truck and drive forever. For three weeks I had felt movement, anticipated a new beginning, but now, I was headed back. And, on the way back, the counting led me to the number I had been fleeing from and inching toward.

At age eleven I quit praying for my father and mother to get back together. When he would visit us he was fragrant and complimentary when my sister or I showed intelligence or wit. But that wasn't often. I remember we competed to make him laugh. We were so eager to have him like us and when he visited we were all on display. In our tiny apartment, with fabric panels as room dividers he would visit us, always in September, always bringing delicious apples. And that's all we would talk about. How crisp they were, how he had picked out the perfect ones, showing us exactly how that was done. We joined in his self-flattery and won some praise. Our mother, dressed up and trying to look slimmer, kept busy. Sweet and efficient. I remember thinking it was probably all her fault our father left us. During those visits my mother had my loyalty, my father had my heart. And that heart so full of love for this unknown presence, would swell and break when he left, and finally it calloused over. So, at age eleven, when prayers and questions failed to produce even the possibility of what I wanted, I got right into bed and simply said, "Never mind".

We didn't see him much until we were older. My sister and I were invited to go to the town where he lived for a visit with him. Nine, ten, eleven, twelve. Thirteen.

I was thirteen, still in love with him, beginning to be me, and he touched me. Late one night, he called me from the hallway after I had used the bathroom, called me over to his chair to sit on his lap and talk to him. I leaned against his broad warm chest and felt his arms holding me close. I was so happy. And then he touched me. He touched me where it all begins, he gave to me and took from me my girl-woman's heart. With that touch there was an invisible seizure and then a pinching howling twist of heart break. This was not right, but the yearning was triggered. And a terrible shame. I know now he would have told me he loved me and taken my body right there, stolen that first sexual experience right from my thirteen year old body. But his wife's car door slammed in the garage and I leapt off his lap.

I was scared suddenly, like Eve in the Garden of Eden, I saw I was naked in a new body. The first man I loved damaged and betrayed me and never said another word about it.

So, the counting stopped. After I came to the number thirteen.

"Over"

One slim paper
tucked in an old book
with a deliberate, fluid
almost moving arrow
that pointed to the far margin.
A helpful "over" rode the arrow down.
On the other side were these words:
"Use this if you want. It is impossible for me to finish."
I took the book home.

OPEN THE DOOR OF YOUR LONGING

Open the door of your longing
to the place where things as yet unmade are fading.

If you hurry you can catch the last glimpse,
the rustle, the sigh of all the dreams that waited
but have already blossomed and died.

First Sight

Mother's new teaching position took us from the lush rhododendron dells and soft-petaled dogwoods of Southwestern Washington to the high country above the Columbia River Gorge. Sharing the co-pilot job, my sister and I unfolded the Mobile Oil map from the glove box and traced the roads we would follow to the new town. After a little arguing and map shaking, we were able to tell our mother: go straight on this road, turn left at Vancouver, go a little ways further and then turn left up into the hills. But no red and blue line on a map prepared me for my first sight of the Columbia River. Rather than taking my breath away, its shimmering blue seemed to force more air into my lungs. Traveling up the Washington side I barely blinked as we went through small towns, the curving pavement taking us up and out of sight and then bringing us back down until we were nearly level with the water. We were in a strange and new landscape of treeless golden buttes, toothy with rim rock, covered in dry sages and late summer flowers I had never seen. So we headed to our new home, thrilling when our mother would honk the horn in the tunnels, looking down on bridges and tiny-looking earth movers working toward building a new dam. When our mother told us we were almost there, I was still turned around in the back seat, the sheer cliffs lost from sight, hoping for one more glimpse of the River.

I wonder now if among the many things we're adding to pollute our land and water, perhaps we are also withholding a more powerful ingredient: remembering our love at first sight, and at least once, returning to it.

Jazz Club

I see a lot of trees
from where I sit.
A tall slender holly
clutching one low group
of bright berries
like a cheap red plastic purse.
Deodora cedar
that even in the slightest breeze
seems to be shyly caught in
her first curtsey.
And then the tall bamboo
that crests over the neighbor's house.
Contact improv dancers
that reach over and bang each other
as though any wind blares
hot jazz.
In the middle of the night
when the wind chimes riot
I picture the tall dancers
with moonlight strobe
and I am not surprised
on waking
that the bamboo looks sleepy.

CAMPTOWN RACES

The mechanic visiting our school was a whistler. As he worked he gave us all a tuneless wheeze that did have a rhythm, a cadence and to all of us watching as he worked, it was known to be a real song. We knew it best at the chorus. Do Da Do Da Day. The first notes were sucked over the bottom teeth on the inhale, the chorus on the exhale. No notes, just punctuated air that fooled us all into hearing a tune and we would feel skippy and jaunty as we left him working under the hood of the old school bus. We were all new missionaries of Camptown Races, swelling with the first song we would one day learn to whistle.

THAW

Snowman:
a lump of snow
and a carrot
with no place to go.

Coveting

The field where I parked the car and walked was well known to me. Miles away a ranch nestled in a grove of shading trees. Ten thousand acres my friend's family owned. Their house sat on a raised plot surrounded by neatly fitted stones, and a green lawn drank smugly beneath the only trees for miles. My friend's mother would check on her cats before she went outside in the heat of summer; if the cats were dozing in the shade, she went about her business to the coop or shed. If the cats were tail-twitching and restless, she would carry her rifle. Rattlesnakes sought the cool stones. Everyone on the ranch had a snakeskin hat band. I really coveted one but one day changed that, like seeing boxes of arrowheads or still and lifeless baskets.

On a weekend visit, I got to ride with the cowboys, out through the gates and up into the high pastures to bring some cattle down. The rubbing of leather against cloth, the clink of bit and shod foot against hard rock, and the blowing of the horses; my memory has never lost the vividness of that afternoon. No conversation that I remember. Just sounds and the heart swelling glee that I was out there, sitting on a saddle, part of something which was not remotely part of my life. A gift.

Two horses ahead of me reared and banged their rumps sideways, and spun in tight reverse turns guided by their riders. The rider in front of me shouted "Back!", not to me but to my horse, and she expertly backed down the trail. I was simply something sitting on her back and could not have done anything to override that command. There was a loud ringing clap, that seemed to come from inside my head, and I felt the flinch of my horse. It was the first gunshot I had ever heard. In a quick dismount, one of the riders grabbed the writhing headless snake. My friend beamed me a huge smile and pointed to her hat. This dead thing was intended for me. Our numbers startling to its own mode of warning or defense had cost it its life. One of the riders, having seen it did what they always did. Had we taken another trail how much longer would that snake have covered the land, fingering each stone and scrubby branch with its belly. My friend stared at me, puzzled by my dismay. Her only way to answer me was to shrug and say: "It's just a snake".

I Would Know You Better

I would know you better
as we are bound
a shade of divine fidelity
together we came
one forgetting
one constant

A Cradle Song

A cradle song
that sings, why me?
This new thing she rocked
cost her all that she loved.
So many first melodies
score our lives.
Every tune we hum
feels like our own,
like a blister
rubbed to life on new skin.

Age's Dream

Where did I go?
There are memories of stars and storms,
days peeled into nights, wrapped in slow motion smiles,
blurred and turning.
The inhale of my breath going in with the autumn, crying,
blown out as winter, laughing,
whispering spring's green damp,
set fierce by summer's sun.
Shapes behind my head, my hair wet with rain,
capped by snow,
sun-drenched, dark strands that lift with a step that takes a year.
Tears fall and dry, laughter creases my cheeks,
as my eyes, season over season,
watch for someone far ahead.
Steps rising and falling, one slow stride,
gaining straightness and speed.
And where I was,
seawater has washed a thousand upon thousand times,
snow that capped my hair has fallen a thousand upon thousand times,
rain that has soaked my shoulders and hands
has fallen a thousand upon thousand times,
and there,
in the blink of an eye who I was moves into view.
My face, my hair, my arms, my hands, my feet
alive and striding past
in the blink of an eye
Where did I go?

FRACTIONS

My mother taught me
to count by tens
and then to subtract
accordingly.
Fractions, of course
had no entry point.
They could not be cumulatively added
and then subtracted
accordingly.
What was I to do with one-third,
two-fifths, five-sevenths?
They brought such chaos.
Imagine then
how I felt
the day I realized
I was living a fraction of my life.

Pick Me

In her seven-year-old body
she rages with noise,
but remains obediently quiet.
She has been told that she is studious, serious,
a backward compliment of comparison.
She is the older one, the quiet one.
No one knows of her racing, fluttering heart
that yearns to things unspoken or the blood
that storms her ears when she wants to cry.
The sidewalk artist beckons the two sisters forward.
"Which of you would like me to draw a picture of you?"
Ah, the younger one beside her,
the twig of laughing curls, bounds forward.
She has been told that she is vivacious,
a joy to all, a bubbly, happy light.
No one knows that she longs for words
that would soothe and seam her little pink heart
of its fears, of its dreams where she is stranded,
when some need of her light fails.
She primps her hair and walks toward the artist.
Her solemn, older sister waits and watches, thinks,
but never says,
"Pick me."

Inkwell of Light

Inkwell of light
her mirror
just as she left it
face down in its room of dark lace
the pewter back
raised and patterned and thumb-shined
where she held it to be sure the faceted brooch
did no harm to the pale silk lapel.
All that she had seen that day
was drawn from her eyes
into its depth
and sketched upon its memory
the mirror's only life
her face.

The Road Home

The road follows the river,
shaving close to its banks
bumps at the edges
of asphalt shaken off,
cooled clots of tar.
Its surface shadowed by trees
and littered with their skin.
Up the hill, past the lawn mowers
blocking a driveway,
Selma's chickens are loose,
pecking and wandering,
drawn by the evergreen shade,
finding bugs, clawing and flapping
against low branches and leggy roots.
Sometimes one or two will get stuck or lost,
until the evening mist from the river
sends its tickling fingers up under the
arch of wing, cold nails against the
still warm wishbone.
And Selma seems to know
banging the back screen door, shaking a small can
saying "Here chicky, chicky" and they all cross
the road and go home.

Weather Change

I changed the weather today.
Gurus say outer reflects inner.
So I wrote a sentence after hot afternoon confinement,
my muscles stacked against my shoulders,
and there was a vibration
a great sulfurous match dragged against
my ribs
right at the longing point
to strike noise and flame from my pen.
It rained.

Shipyard Lunch

The only colors seemed to be rust and gray. There were walkways and ladders everywhere, sprays of welding sparks, pneumatic hisses, and small looking humans hammering and hammering against the echoing ship hulls. Below where I stood, I could see a drive shaft and propeller, shiny brass and altogether the size of a building. There were three men up there moving around the wings of the propeller but they didn't seem to touch it. Above them was the notch where it would go, shaft, propeller, the master and servant, stranded in this dry dock. Here was no cold lapping water, just hoses connected to oxyacetylene tanks, and no seaweed, just wires leading to hooded men with sparking hands.

    A whistle blew, barely audible through the hiss and hammer blows, but as one, many men halted, turned off their torches, reached for green or gray or blue metal pails, climbed up the ladders, and out of the pits. I followed them. My pail was black and scuffed with sprung lock-down clamps; the handle was loose and clicked against my leg. The stairs zigzagged up, gray marine enamel painted on everything. At the top I emerged behind the men when one man stopped and sat to the side of the stairs. More men moved past but he just sat where he was. In a gray-green jumpsuit, wearing heavy, dark brown wear-blistered boots, he stretched out his legs and raised the welder's helmet visor from his face. The instant pink of his skin dazzled my eyes, and his light, sky blue eyes startled me. Floating between red inflamed lids, their wet rims looked close to spilling over, like someone about to cry but all he did was look off into the distance, blinking. With his grime-gloved hand he opened the green pail, pulled out a red-topped thermos, and a bagged sandwich. The last I saw of him was the flash of white teeth as he took the first bite of a roast beef sandwich, stained pink, the color of his shipyard lunch.

Detour

There was a detour I took one day.
It crossed a tiny piece of fertile valley.
For a moment I did not know what I was seeing.
Acres of pear trees cut down, recent to this winter day,
laying like chevrons of silver on the scuffed valley soil.
Again in March I passed that way
and saw a haze of pink and white upon each tree.
They were blooming.
The life force fierce and contained
followed the only course it knew.
They were blooming, severed
yet so strong with life they couldn't be stopped
from being what they are.
Acres of blooms,
dreaming of the groaning weight of past fruit.

River Walker

A buck was wading in the glittering, cold river. Straight down the middle of its gouged surface, gouged with a wood carver's symmetry, the dimples repeating and staying in place as the current moved. The rushing water was the grain. Did the lifted foot of the walking deer change the bottom as well as the water? Were new patterns formed as gravel filled in a hoof print, changing the river all the way to the sea? The deer moved slowly mid-stream, the water licking at its chest and high flank, alert ears funneling in sound over the chug and clack of the rock bed and creaking bare branches on the bank. A slight stumble was corrected and the deer just stepped on, royally, like a pharaoh winked into a new dimension, just stepped on toward the next deep run as the river snaked around a giant tree that hung down over the water. I carefully stood to walk the few yards to watch. The old tree stretched and bobbed across the river's path; I was sure the buck had to go another way. The empty waving branches formed eye-confusing patterns, like foil confetti in sunlight. Reason and sight argue with what is solid, what is open and then "Snap," I saw the rhythmic movement of antlers as the shoulder moved forward a step, down the center of the river, on the other side of the tree. I stood and watched until the forest colors of gray and brown once more folded a kind of blindness over my eyes. I picked up my coat and coffee and knew I could never imagine that buck leaving the center of the river, stepping slowly, leading a procession through all the shapes and shades of gray water. If it had bounded away I would have noticed and forgotten it, but the measured steps down the river, seemingly through that rock-a-bye tree, helped me imagine it was still going. A dreamed creature of some other being, intercepted by me, tethering me to their dream.

Get Out of My Way

Through the badlands of Idaho there is a highway
with signs that point to towns named Dickshooter, Dry Forty
and Fairylawn,
signs that tell me I am in Owyhee County,
signs that confirm I am going as fast
as four cylinders can take me,
to new rooms and away from old ones.
The hood and windshield are fuzzy with moth parts
painted with iridescent smears
and still more fill my headlights.
It is here on this high road
when distance finally pinches the radio signal
from wavy ghost voices to choking static that I am alone
without human sound to fill the stretching, silent, warm,
violet dark.
Then, from that straight drawn-out note of road in front of me,
a song comes into me,
and this song has some muscle
and begins to push into those inner spaces
where just beneath the radio chatter
crowds of old memories have been milling around.
My song begins to blow outward,
past the headlights, snagging like low fog
on tall sage and rabbit grass.
Straight ahead I can imagine the shapes of those who closed in
tight around me,
not to protect but to confine,
like they can sense my in-breath they rush toward me,
and singing I crash through them.
Nothing can contain this new music from me
and I sing full out with the tires, the moths, the pebbled black,
and all of my words are big-fisted and purple.

Asylum

In her mind she can see the letters
swimming, flying, looping.
In her mind words take shape
form spider webs, their holes woven together.
In her mind,
even when her feet look like cat paws,
and her hands look like hooves,
and others come to look at her
and move their lips like fish,
in her mind only verse and rhyme.
She struggles to see the lawn and the fawn
Reaches to see the sky and the pie
before the needle stings her dark again
when all the letters flutter to the brown tile floor.

GLIMPSES

We think we see everything we look at
but it is just a part
we see the top, the side
oh, the whole is there
but our sight shatters from too much light.
We see the bars of a cage
looking solid and rigid
but they are only lines we think should be there.
What waits for us to blink or move to the side,
one inch, two?
While we stand fixed,
satisfied with glimpses of open fields
from behind the bars of a cage.

Following

"She ran naked. There."
Who has just spoken? Pointed?
A bent and wrinkled old man
with mussed hair and baggy clothes.
No one wants to look at him.
His lips are still moving as he drifts away,
like a wad of brown paper puffed at by wind.
He had been a brave boy
but could never boast
because the day
she ran naked, he followed her,
the image of her body like a locket
pressed against his own breast.
And so he hid
and watched as she became the forest floor to the
lover that waited in the grove for her.
Shuffling away now
his old fingers touch where his heartache curled into a corpse.
"She ran naked."
There.

CHRYSALIS

Out of the confining
gleaming nylon
of the tent
out with the wet wings of waking woman,
I looked down past the slashed
layered rock to the mercury
shimmer of the Colorado.
Grand. Canyon. Dawn.

Lost & Found

From my favorite seat at the library I can see so many things.
The table is a pale wood that matches the straight, hard chair, both looking
like they should be so much heavier.
But I have to scoot and scoot to get my elbows and pens and notebook
to somehow meet as they were meant.
The passing traffic below occasionally relieves my tired eyes,
the clouds and their shadows across the valley guide the fleeting deeper thought.
Today it is late May and the blooms of bright flowers are starting to hang out of the planters
shading the street corners with purple and yellow,
colors priming the dark asphalt for summer paint.
Every Tuesday, I watch that man with his singlar rustic plowman's stride,
pushing his grocery cart, wrapped in shiny black plastic, mounded with his harvest
of tin cans and brittle bottles.
Just now, a child in a dark parka,
wearing pink and green polka dot tights and red cowboy boots
dances up the library steps. She looks up at my window seat.
Does she see me?
I glance at the lost-and-found rack and it is full of coats and hats.
Who walked away without that bright green sweater?
And that hat, wouldn't you think you would know right away that something was missing?
My notebooks are like that.
I open to begin going backward or forward, and wonder
how I walked away from that bright sentence,
and when I left that paragraph out,
shouldn't I have known right away something was missing?

Sunday's Best

I remember the smell of the church basement on Sunday, the smell of the ladies guild kitchens' carrying their aromas to church; cinnamon, cream, banana, allspice; the splash of punch on white paper doilies, butter cream on the pastor's tie, my grandmother's gladiolas straight and true in tall baskets near the door.

I remember the smell of brewed coffee years before I would taste it, burping in bright metal urns with a napkin under the spigot to quickly catch the pour spout drip. I remember the sugar cubes and taking three from the ceramic flower-shaped dish, watched carefully by the hosting ladies, the way wary hens might watch a strolling cat. Their glances just enough to remind me not to be messy or greedy or rude in the presence of such obvious generosity. Glances that stayed on the shoulders like raindrops.

I remember dark suits and shiny shoes and hands damp from being dressed up too long or in church too long or from shyness on display. I remember the small glass plates with the tea-cup lip on the side and how they were quickly gathered and washed and dried and tucked into the silent cupboards; the pride of Sunday's best. I remember going home, sweet sugar still on my teeth and lips, changing clothes and dancing while everyone else took a nap.

The Library Steps

The little girl is dressed in her costume of the day.
A blue scarf falls to her knees,
held in place by a sequin piled pin,
a white skirt, stiff and bouncy
and Oh, those red sparkling shoes
flat to the ground but designed to elevate
common to royal.
She chooses each step to descend,
her bearing regal.
Then she pauses on a step and carefully toes something down,
a large bug or stone or burdened bumblebee, or
maybe all that's left
of a squirrel-chewed pine cone.
She gently slides it down the last two steps
nudges it to the center square of sidewalk, and
STOMPS it flat,
moves it again and STOMPS
and kicks what's left into the street.
Two skips ahead and she is out of sight
holding the hand of her mother,
ice cream next.
So I wonder,
what in her path,
on that most common library step
called to her for its destruction from her passing?

Workshop

"Poetry is the vibration that stirs the soul."
That is Paul talking, for once using words
that almost everyone knows.
Martha chimes in, offering her knowledge that
poetry is the deep water of life, flowing through us as words.
I should have left at the break, my mind already truant.
Lists of words on colored paper,
warranted to ignite genius.
Trees bow outside the tall narrow windows.
I cap my pen.
There is some deep, deep confession riding high
on my tear ducts; I must have the good grace to
attend to it soon.
I wonder if there was a word on that list
I should have written down.

Yoo-Hoo!

First look at the river this morning
and the walkers below me.
Each mind full of thoughts
winking through bright matter.
Like the sea gulls coasting low
each wing beat playing with the light of instinct.
But no one is looking up.
Imagination flies quietly.

The Snyders' Goat

I loved the smell of that goat.
Oh, but I didn't go sniffing its manure, no,
I loved the smell of the goat when I hugged her neck.
Like my cat, or the neighbor's old farm horse, or my
grandmother's coat.
Some smells are so truly particular that eyes aren't necessary.
How many goat necks have I smelled? Cats? Horses?
Probably not enough for the sample of scientific truth, but I
know it is true.
Everyone else said, "Pew," and hurried back toward the house.
But I always stayed.
There in the barn were other wonderful smells.
I could smell the dust from the rusted spikes in the beams
and posts, the rimed leather harness pieces,
the damp smell the chickens brought in,
the stirred up old straw dust that floated down
across the vacant stalls.
High in the barn roof
shingles in ones and twos had abandoned the heavy beams,
sliding to the straw below or in the wind
back to the forest edge,
where the cedar pores of each shingle sighed
back home, back home.
Small birds deepened each timber corner
with wide-mouthed nests,
layering them with more pieces of straw or grass
or horse tail hair.
Moonlight, starlight, rain, frost, snow, dust,
all made the old barn their home
and somehow combined,
in a July sunbeam,
coating the neck of that goat
for me to smell.

Running with Robert

Robert came out, went down the steps and started his run, heading down the street, around the corner, and was soon out of our sight. I worried that it was a mistake to let Juneau watch him run away. She raised her head, ears and eyes focused as he turned the corner and for a moment I thought she would slowly get to her feet and try to follow. Speaking her name, I touched her head and rubbed at her ears.

"No," I said softly, "you stay here with me."

Without taking her eyes off the street, she settled back to the worn porch deck, probably even then, she was hearing his distant foot falls.

Within the heart of a dog, no matter the age, the desire to run is always ready, an electrical current switched on by a whistle, a clap or the unmistakable promise of "let's go." It is a passionate, get-sick-without-it desire. And because of that she would have followed him in her stiff, rolling, sixteen-year-old gait. But I know that she is running too. She runs beside or ahead of him, never behind. Her stride is long and low, wolfy. New brighter blood massages her heart and she feels each leaf and pebble on the pavement. Her ears and nose, triggered by instinct and ancestry know there have been two raccoons right there, that the cat Hercules pounced on something in that tuft of grass, a crow bounce-walked off to the left. All of this she holds within that slim aging body of soft hair, yellow teeth and tender feet.

So, she's running with Robert right now, lying against my feet, watching the street. It was not a mistake to let her see him out of sight and when he comes back, she'll come inside and take a great long drink of water. She has run with him before and like a favorite dream, she will run with him each day, the energy ripe blood will fill her heart, and while we wait for him on the porch, the breeze will carry her heartbeat.

I Brought Back Sounds

After walking through the forest
I brought back sounds.
In my hair, in my shirt, stuck in the treads of my shoes.
My steps were noisy
so my shoes gathered up gravel and tough twig pieces.
From my shirt
the sound of hidden falling water
and a frog's description of a May afternoon.
In my hair
there was birdsong, bough whispers,
yellow sunspots on wide green leaves.
All around me and pressing on my skin
were the sounds of my forest walk.
I cannot carry the earth
but still she wraps me in the sounds
she loves
so I listen
and she says
"Come back."

Tsunami

Wanting to be here this morning
thinking our gaze would soothe the ocean turmoil.
But sadness companions our walk.
Can I just look
without seeing that far-away blackness
where just days ago
people died by the thousands?
I want to go deep, deep to its soiled floor,
the way some want to rush into
a burning building.
Oh, this beautiful sea where
now beyond the gasping tide
other creatures
mid-song, mid-gaze are gloved by our waste.
Imagining I can feel the blistered earth
beneath our feet, see whales floating
down in cold darkness.
And then the breeze stirs the dune grasses,
little shore birds wink in and out of the surf,
gulls kite back out to the waves,
and our dog runs joyfully back to us,
loving who she sees.

Marilyn

The dress she wore was once red with small clusters of faded blue flowers patterned throughout the limp worn cloth. Small and pale, standing straight with her feet planted defiantly in her heavy farm boots, she gripped the chalk tray beneath the black board. A fume of bleach and urine followed her into the room. There was a rapid scraping of chair legs against the slick linoleum then a twitter from Denny, who did an exaggerated nose itch. She looked directly at me. I looked away. So, Marilyn standing there, was already forming as a wound in my memory. Standing there watching all of us without a friend in sight.

River Paths

Paths that wander along the river
deliberately lead to muck
and mire
and reeds
and shelves of gnats and dragonflies.
The paths are charged with keeping the river
always slightly out of range.
Paths that wander along the river
are shy lovers
they can only lie beside
and never enter
without losing themselves.

DECLARATIONS

I have driven through a storm in Northern Idaho
with a bald eagle riding shotgun.
I saw a crow fall dead to the street
in the town of Twisp.
I have heard the sun roar, facing a cliff at sunrise.
I lost a watch and two shoes in a dark pond
where I rescued the drowning Red Dog.
I have hurt kind men.
I have loved to gain favor.
I have lost many times.
I have heard a cedar tree
talk,
to me.

River of Permission

It is breathlessly hot. No breeze bends or raises the blades of grass or drooping leaves. To inhale is like taking deep breaths of hot fog. But you have found it. Flowing just feet away. Deep, dark green water. Brief pity for the thirsty trees, the baking, crumbling rocks. For you now, each step toward the fluttering edge is taken with relief. Before water even touches a toe, you already feel the coolness enclosing your ankles, your shoulders. Before you even enter the water you know the taste of this river. Stepping like one descending a stair, feet, ankles, knees in exaggerated but precise steps you yield to the muscular wetness of current. The strength of it surprises you and then the green water has encased your chest. One more step and only your face is untouched by the river. A hesitation, a breath and the water closes over your head, pulling your hair and bubbling in your ears. Nothing to see or hear, only feel, finally feel the sensation you imagined, feel the urge to lie back and let the thick legs of water carry you away. All is trust and willingness. But this deep water holds other things. Something you did not foresee or imagine.

Lightning hits your nerve endings and all your surface textures say escape, and your brain willingly pulls the trigger on the weapon of fear. Joints no longer longing to be immersed now clack and splay to be free of this murky, pushing darkness. The rocks and trees may know what is in these depths, but you don't. And you decide you can go no further. You flee. You tear your heart out of the fierce water. You have escaped back into your life for something never seen or known. Only imagined. The same way you imagined its embrace.

We are the ones who have to keep going back to the river. Who have to keep having to flee and talk about the trip. Come with me into the river and let that chill and darkness take you where you and only you are supposed to go. Act defiantly with your courage but befriend your fear. It can embolden you. It can destroy you. But quitting is no less an imaginary act than succeeding.

Acknowledgements

Christi Payne, Page & Book, designed and edited this book and has guided it from my hands to yours.

Thank you to all my family, friends, and teachers and the town of my heart, Astoria.

Cover art by Robert Paulmenn.